W9-AYC-751

WOODY, BE GOOD!
A First Book of Manners

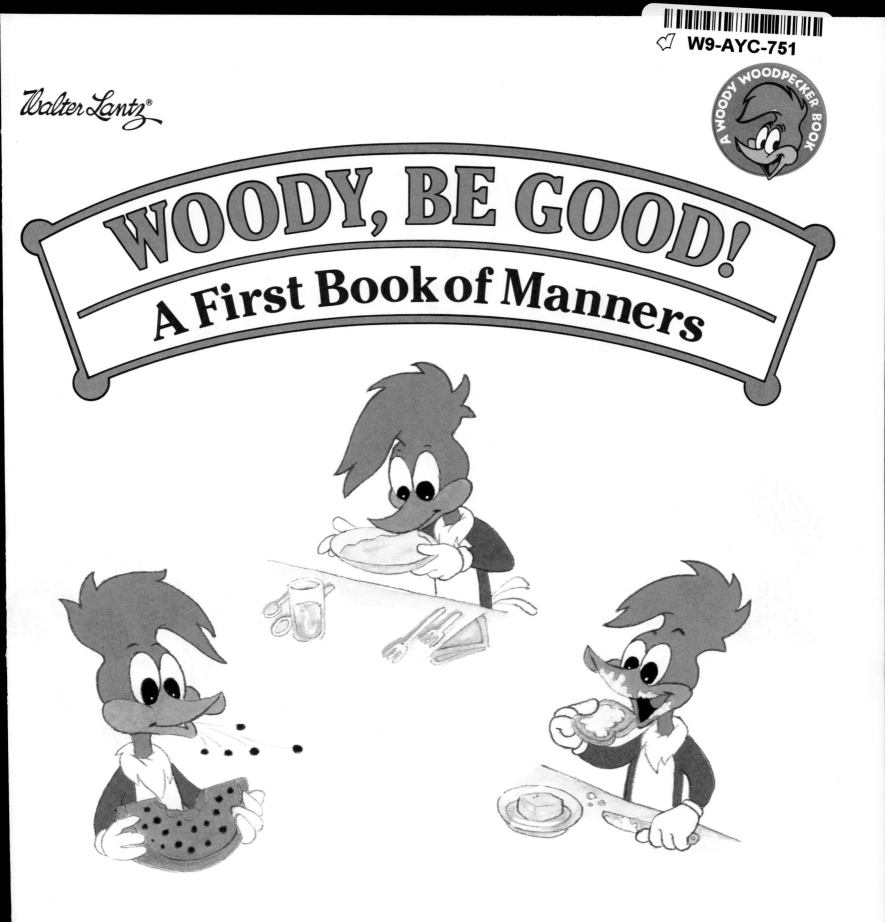

By Margo Lundell • Illustrated by Eve Rose

PUBLISHERS • GROSSET & DUNLAP • NEW YORK

Did Someone Mention Manners?

Woody Woodpecker and his pals are a friendly bunch, but they sometimes forget their manners.

What are manners? They are the way people behave. To have good manners, you need to learn some simple rules. But good manners are more than just rules. Good manners have to do with people being kind and considerate to each other. Someone who always bullies or pokes fun does not think about other people's feelings. That person does not have good manners.

Woody and his friends can use a brush-up on good behavior. Let's hope they remember what they learn!

Mannerly Words

May I please try on your hat, Uncle Woody?

Hey, give me that hat!

Please Say Please

When you ask for something, always say **please**. It's a magic word that makes everything go more smoothly.

Thank you, Uncle Woody!

And Please Say Thank You

Be sure to say **thank you** whenever someone does something for you. Hearing a polite **thank you** makes people feel good.

Excuse Me

When people are talking, try not to interrupt. If you have to speak, say **excuse me**. That's the polite way to get someone's attention.

> Hey, guys. Guess who made the front page?

> Oh! Excuse me, Homer!

Meeting New People

When you meet a person for the first time, introduce yourself and shake hands.

> How do you do? I'm Charlie Beary.

Saying **excuse me** is also a way to say **I'm sorry**.

Getting Along with People

Be cheerful: When you see someone, say *hello*. Everyone likes to be noticed.

Be cooperative: If someone asks you to do some work, pitch in without a fuss.

Be helpful: If you see work that needs doing, ask if you can help.

Respect others: If someone has worked hard, don't mess up his good work.

Be generous and share: Don't hog things.

Respect other people's property: Don't break someone else's toy. Don't borrow anything without asking permission.

On the Telephone

Hello, this is Chilly Willy.
May I speak to the furnace fixer?

Calling

When you call someone, say **hello**, give your name, and ask for the person you want to talk to.

Hello.... Just a minute, please.
I'll see if Mr. Hot can come to the phone.

THE HOT SPOT

Answering

When you answer the phone, say **hello** in a friendly voice. If the call is not for you, tell the caller to wait while you get the person.

Mr. Hot can't come to the phone right now. May I take a message?

Taking a Message

If the person is busy or not there, take a message. If you can, write the message down. Be sure to include:

1. the name of the person who called
2. the time of the call
3. what the caller said
4. his or her number.

Chilly Willy called at 10:00 A.M. He needs his furnace fixed. Call him at 555-5555.

Mealtime

At Home

Dinnertime! It's polite to wait until everyone is seated before you begin to eat.

Be careful about reaching. If you can't reach something, ask someone else to get it for you. Saying **please pass it** is often the best way to get what you need.

Suzy, wait for your father!

Mealtime Do's and Don'ts

Do pass food **around** the table—not across.

Do keep your elbows tucked in at the table.

Do try new foods. You may like them—and you'll make the cook happy.

Do put your knife and fork squarely in the middle of the plate when you are finished eating.

Don't talk with your mouth full and **don't** chew with your mouth open.

Don't tuck your napkin under your chin. Place it on your lap.

Don't use your fingers to push food on your fork. Use your knife or a piece of bread instead.

Don't lean on the table or tip your chair back.

I'm starved!

Eating Out

When you go to a restaurant, let the host lead you to your table.

In a fancy restaurant, you may feel bewildered. Which spoon should you use? Which fork should you use?

The trick is knowing that the fork or spoon on the outside is the one to use first. The teaspoon goes outside the soup spoon because it may be used for the fruit cup, which is usually served before the soup.

The short salad fork comes first because salad is often served before the main course. The long fork to the right of the salad fork is used next—it is the dinner fork.

How to Eat It

Bread: Break off and butter one bite-sized piece at a time.

Soup: Dip the spoon away from you.

Catsup: Pour it alongside the meat or potatoes.

Watermelon: Eat watermelon with a knife and fork and don't spit the seeds across the table.

May I be excused?

Before You Go

Before you leave the table, it's important to say **May I be excused**?

Party Time

Giving a Party

As the host, it is your job to greet your guests at the door. Tell each one that you are glad he or she could come. If it is a birthday party, say thank you for the gifts.

Welcome, Woody!

Serve food to your guests before you serve yourself. Being a host means thinking about others.

Going to a Party

If you're a guest, make sure you say **hello** to the host and also to her parents.

Being a guest means being on your best behavior—at the table and elsewhere. Roughhousing is not appreciated!

Sleepovers

When a Friend Spends the Night

If you're the host, it's your job to make your guest comfortable. Show your friend where to put his belongings and where he will sleep.

Here's where you can hang up your stuff, Maxie.

I usually watch TV until 2 A.M.

If You're the Guest

When you spend the night at a friend's house, obey his house rules about watching television, going to bed, and other things.

Taking Good Care of a Friendship

Do stand by a friend.
Do keep your promises to him.
Do tell a friend the truth.
Do encourage and praise a friend.

Don't make fun of a friend.
Don't be a tattletale.
Don't yell at a friend—but it's OK to disagree.
Don't do all the talking. A friend is a good listener.

School Days

Arriving at School

It's polite to say **good morning** to your teacher.

In the Classroom

Be as friendly as you can with everyone at school. Even if you don't like someone, you can still be polite.

Waiting in Line

Wait your turn at the water fountain or the pencil sharpener. Nobody likes to be pushed out of line.

At Gym Class

Be a good sport. If you win, do not brag. If you lose, don't whine. There's always a next time.

Can Oswald stay and play, Pop?

When you have a guest over, try to be neat. Don't leave the kitchen messy or toys and books lying around for someone else to clean up.

After School

Don't invite a friend home after school without checking with your parents and his.

Going Places

In the Park

Enjoy yourself in the park. Be careful not to litter or do anything that would hurt the plants or trees.

At the Movies

When you go to the movies, a play, or a concert, you sometimes have to squeeze by others to get to your seat. Face people as you walk past and say **excuse me**.

HA HA HA HA HA!

A Travel Tip

When you travel be sure to keep your voice low. On a train or an airplane or in other close quarters, even normal talk sounds loud.

Wow! Look at that alligator!

GATOR SWAMP

Car Courtesy

Long car trips can be hard on everyone. Even so, a passenger should make himself think about the driver. Leaning on the driver or shouting in her ear, for example, won't help her drive safely.

Farewell, Feathered Friend

Our woodpecker manners book
    is cheerfully done,
and our Woody is chasing
    the red setting sun.

What a wacky young bird!
    Can he possibly learn
how to slow himself down
    or wait for his turn?

Dear Woody, be good
    and remember to write.
Be kind to your neighbor—
    and also polite!